Church Girl On A Regular Basis: Church Girl Takes High School

MAJAYLA PAGE

CHURCH GIRL ON A REGULAR BASIS: Church Girl Goes Takes High School

Copyright © 2020 Majayla Page

All rights reserved.

ISBN: 9798676641689

Cover picture purchased from Canva.com 8/3/2020

Scriptures from the Holy Bible are used in this manuscript.

CHURCH GIRL ON A REGULAR BASIS: Church Girl Goes Takes High School

Dedication

This book is dedicated to the one that said, "You can do this Jay." Thank you, mommy.

CHURCH GIRL ON A REGULAR BASIS: Church Girl Goes Takes High School

CHURCH GIRL ON A REGULAR BASIS: Church Girl Goes Takes High School

ACKNOWLEDGMENTS

I want to first acknowledge God, who is the Head of my life. Where will I be without my Creator? Jesus saved me at an early age, and I want my life to be a light for Him. Ecclesiastes 12:1 says, "Remember now thy Creator in the days of thy youth..." I'm grateful for my parents and my brother! You all are the treasures of my heart. I wouldn't be me without God using you to birth me into this earth, but who continues to nurture and train me in the ways of God, so that I can be a productive citizen in this earth! I'm grateful for my Pastor, who has been a cornerstone since I could remember! Your teachings, prayers, and wisdom shared are not in vain!

CHURCH GIRL ON A REGULAR BASIS: Church Girl Goes Takes High School

Before you start……

As you read through this book, I really want you to know that God is BIGGER than any problems! Zits are temporary, friends come, and it's ok to let them go….and yes, you CAN make it!

CHURCH GIRL ON A REGULAR BASIS: Church Girl Goes Takes High School

Intro:

1:38 pm

Ring- Ring- Ring- Rrrringg!! There's Brittany – brown hair, pale skin, black glasses, black boots, jeans, and golden earrings, a black top, and a purple scarf – who's our future lawyer walking down the hall. "Wow she's changed since middle school," I think to myself. And then there's me, the world future Christain entertainer. The girl who's on her way to heaven and happy about it.

Walking into the band room, the last class of the day (aka: the make or break mission: "Hold on, until you hear the bell." "Hey Sunshine", I say brightly to Andre. Can't help but smile, he says in the lowest voice, "Hey Majayla." A girl giggles, in a corner, while a boy plays on her tummy. Cussing rises in the instrument storage room. Yes, I am

CHURCH GIRL ON A REGULAR BASIS: Church Girl Goes Takes High School

your future world changer and leader, but I have to jump this herald called High School!

I'm saved, and Holy Ghost filled and now in High School. Being saved did not admit me from the chaos of teen life, nor the drama that comes with high school. But I'm here to tell you that no matter what happens, with God, you can make it!

CHURCH GIRL ON A REGULAR BASIS: Church Girl Goes Takes High School

CHAPTER 1

An hour has passed and I've seen the cruelest thing! After playing the marching band show, all of a sudden the class falls silent. As I raise my head, I see the teacher running to take a picture of a boy slumped over in his chair in perfect sleep. Students gather around with their phones out taking pictures too. I felt bad and tried to say wake up but lord he was too gone. With the weakest voice and smile.

The teacher says, "Where's the leadership?" I deeply feel that as believers our faith is tested in high school because it began to change and find themselves. Not to mention your hormones and peer pressure. I mean the day before yesterday took a turn! While In my favorite class, which is Dance class, I noticed that whatever I did I heard giggles. Until I heard a girl say "Just ignore her;" I walked near my spot, and I just knew the subject was simply about me. I told

CHURCH GIRL ON A REGULAR BASIS: Church Girl Goes Takes High School

my mom when I got home and I began to rethink things and said, "Maybe she wasn't talking about me because I asked Neshia, and she said that they were not." My mom then said, "God gives us common sense. You know and I know she was talking about you.

She's not in God and when the devil sees the light of truth shining, the devil always aims to dim it!" and that's when I had to make the choice to shine or to dim my new light (my love for Jesus and Holy Ghost). Matthew 5:16 says, " Let your light so shine before men, that they may see your good works, and glorify your Father which is in heaven." Therefore though I already feel shaky and school just started, I will choose to let my light so shine, in this weird place called High school!

CHURCH GIRL ON A REGULAR BASIS: Church Girl Goes Takes High School

CHAPTER 2

Were you ever so frustrated you wanted to cry, and the last word that came in your head was a failure? Well, I'm in that state of being right now. Today, in dance class, was just a red flag. I find it extremely funny that it's always my favorite class. Well, for the first section of the class, it went well; we stretched, talked, and did a run-through of the still-in-progress dance. Then, my teacher called me out to read the moves out of a dance magazine.

I took the book and the girls crowd around me- *'hello is it ok for me to breathe'*, I think to myself. I told a girl to show the movement since she attended a dance school after regular school hours. Most of the girls started to talk about how they didn't understand and even plainly said, "I'm not doing this." They crowded back around me when I constantly said, "Just listen and get back please." Brianna and Kenny – my friends,

CHURCH GIRL ON A REGULAR BASIS: Church Girl Goes Takes High School

supposedly- said repeatedly, 'next', 'ok', 'we got it', and 'thank you'; all sarcastically. Brianna went so far, as to clap to 'make ' me speed up! I then decided to show the moves myself, but that backfired; the girls began to laugh. I became furious, and I felt my face get red. Then, the teacher yelled, "Everyone should be doing this, GET UP!"

Then, the girl that I had to help show the movements, snatched the magazine out of my hand, and fixed her mouth to utter, "Some girls are saying, you're not doing it right, so just let me do it." I guess she was just upset and jealous that the teacher had me teach the dance and not her- typical!

With a stern and steady voice, I said , "No, Mrs. PB told me to do it, so y'all just try it." Another girl then suggested that I turn over the magazine, so the others could see the pictures. I then shut my eyes and took a breath. I then opened my eyes and turned around. "Majayla is doing this because I asked her to," I heard the

CHURCH GIRL ON A REGULAR BASIS: Church Girl Goes Takes High School

teacher shout out. She then softly looks my way, and says, "Just read slowly." I slow down a lot and begin to say things humorous, just to brighten the tension up for me. It didn't get any better, and I got so frustrated that I said, "Oh my gosh, y'all just listen and do it!"

By the sound of it, anyone could have seen that I was at my breaking point! You should have seen the looks on their faces when I said that – They smiled and they were all filled with joy, as if this is what they wanted to happen and to their surprise it did-. I walked over to Mrs. PB and with a calm voice I said, "Mrs. PB I can't do this ."

Then, the girls crowded around my teacher, and I heard them say " .....Yeah until she freaked out." Oh, I 'freaked' out!? And Nia, the most popular girl in school, as she thought- searched for my facial expression. I managed not to cry. ..

CHURCH GIRL ON A REGULAR BASIS: Church Girl Goes Takes High School

But to be honest all my high school journey has not been so bad. There are days when I smile and choose to shake the dust off my feet, no matter what the day brings. Other days one good thing can happen- like me making a 102 on a Biology test – and I'll shout every chance I get with Tye Tribett's song, *"He Turned It"* ringing in my ear. And then there are days like these...

The kind of days that remind you that not everyone is for you and will applaud when you are chosen. Some people want to see you fail, but it is up to you to take the victory with the power we already have or to simply give it away. *Ephesians 3:16–20* James 1:12

CHURCH GIRL ON A REGULAR BASIS: Church Girl Goes Takes High School

CHAPTER 3

"...but God is faithful, who will not suffer you to be tempted above that ye are able." 1 Corinthians 10:13

Today, when I walked to school I met up with Shawn, - an old friend – and he told me he went to a funeral yesterday for the person who had got shot recently. And he was going to another one tomorrow for his cousin. Meanwhile, Renee came to him and said in a whisper "You heard......she died." I walked into the school building and headed to the library.

I dropped my book bag and trumpet on a table and went out the door. Going with my regular routine, I was heading to the dining room to eat breakfast. Then, Deandee (a girl in my dance class), passed by stopping me in tracks, "Hey Jayla," she said brightly, and then whispered, "...Did you hear what happened?"

CHURCH GIRL ON A REGULAR BASIS: Church Girl Goes Takes High School

"What?" I said concerned. "Maddie's momma died, they found her DEAD today."

Maddie Johnson: old childhood friend; sweet; smart; basketball player; pretty; and funny.

We used to be tight during elementary school, and during the after school program. We would laugh at people so much, that the little kids looked at us funny! We now just say 'hey', 'bye', and joke around when we happen to be in the same place.

Dylan Johnson: Brother of Maddie Jonson; funny, crazy, smart, handsome, game-playing, mannered, sweet type of boy.

He used to laugh in my face at the after school program, for no known reason, and that made me and Maddie die laughing! He says 'hey' to me in a funny way and cuts a joke with me here and there with me and has the biggest smile that one has ever seen.

Their mom: Mother of both children; warm sweet understanding; beautiful; and opens her arms to

CHURCH GIRL ON A REGULAR BASIS: Church Girl Goes Takes High School

all. The few times I've spoken and talked with her she was all that and MORE. It all hit me like a ton of bricks. I slid to the side of the hall. Against the wall....I cried saying "Jesus". I couldn't believe it. " It's not that serious", Deandee said. " But it is", I said. My voice cracked with each word. I waved her away and said, "I gotta go". Hugging myself tight, I stormed to the door. I wasn't the only one hurt.

Girls formed in groups to cry and talk. As I walked in the lunchroom, Zyquaisha was knocking over the table. The cafeteria ladies asked why she was crying like that, 'that's not her mom', they said. But they were wrong, we all were hurt. My friends saw that I was low on life, and asked me what was wrong. While explaining I broke down. Most walked out saying I was gonna make them cry.

Walking out of the library, I heard boys say "Man, I can't go anywhere; they're crying in there crying in-". He stopped when he saw me, because I was one of the 'criers'. While I was wiping my tears, Mrs. Heart came to me saying, "You signed up for the vice president and president. You can't do that, which one do you want?" "President please," I struggled to talk. I joined Latasha, Shell, and Shawn at the lockers; almost all of them were crying. All of them are friends with Maddie, but Latasha was Maddie's bestie. Tamara joined us- she plays basketball with her, and the more she talked the more she cried. I cried quietly holding myself, the tears just kept coming.

  Deandee came up next to me holding my arms, I took it as comfort. The bell rang; time for class. We kind of walked in lines, linked by arms. It felt like we were marching in a funeral. I broke away remembering that I left my things in the library. When I entered my homeroom class, Mrs. Jones pointed to me and said, "Dylan is her brother, ain't it?" I nodded. " I knew her, about all her life," she continued. Oddly, I just knew she was talking about Maddie's mom. She stays right down the road from where my father lives," she said. Tears rolled down her face, as she said, "She

CHURCH GIRL ON A REGULAR BASIS: Church Girl Goes Takes High School

was a nice lady....excuse me a minute." She walked out of the classroom quickly after grabbing a Kleenex tissue while wiping her eyes. My crying got worse, I began to make the coughing sounds, and my shoulders began to shake. I don't know, it just happened. I heard someone then say, " Majayla, you ok?". With a fake smile, I said " "I'm ok", forcing myself not to stop crying.

Later that day, I wept in my mother's arms. The whole day was a struggle. This wasn't something I read out a book, nor did I hear it from somewhere else. It was real life, and I just think "I" was complaining about spending thanksgiving at a hospital because my grandpa is having heart surgery. At least he's still alive....at least he's still alive.

CHURCH GIRL ON A REGULAR BASIS: Church Girl Goes Takes High School

CHAPTER 4

Psalm 30: 5 "For his anger is but for a moment, and his favor is for a lifetime. Weeping may tarry for the night, but joy comes with the morning."

"How I got over, You know my soul looks back and wonders how I got over."

A week later, I wrote them a note, for words of encouragement and love- you know how I do! My momma let me give it to them at their house, the day of the funeral; we were heading to NC to see my grandpa at Duke Hospital. I talked with their aunt and told them why I couldn't attend the service.

I was going to ask her to give Maddie and Dylan the note, but all of a sudden Maddie came out to see me. She had a black tank top with a towel around her waist. She seemed to be getting ready for the funeral. Her hair was in a pretty donut bun. "Majayla," she said softly and slightly amazed. She came up to me with arms wide open.

CHURCH GIRL ON A REGULAR BASIS: Church Girl Goes Takes High School

While hugging her, I don't know why but I said, "Hallelujah." In between her hug a dog jumped on my legs. Her aunt said, "That's right baby Hallelujah." With a bright smile, I said 'goodbye' and walked out relieved.

That following week Maddie and Dylan came back to school acting regular. I tried to approach Maddie by saying "Hi," but she wasn't too patient. She got up and walked away but I was ok. I decided to not hold anything against her. Dylan didn't come the first day but that next day he came. When saying 'hey' to him, his smile was not as bright as usual, and his eyes were puffy.

It's December, a new month, new mercy I see. I'm doing better, my grandpa is doing better. I've noticed that Dylan is not hanging out with his nerdy friends, and it worries me a little, but I've decided to let God take care of them both. I thank God because after you've suffered a while, greater will come. High school is not that bad as people say. I guess when you love, accept, trust, and lean and depend on God everything seems to sparkle even at your weakest point.

CHURCH GIRL ON A REGULAR BASIS: Church Girl Goes Takes High School

CHAPTER 5

Romans 12:2 ESV

Do not be conformed to this world, but be transformed by the renewal of your mind, that by testing you may discern what is the will of God, what is good and acceptable and perfect.

Galatians 1:10 ESV / 381 helpful votes
For am I now seeking the approval of man, or of God? Or am I trying to please man? If I were still trying to please man, I would not be a servant of Christ.

It was time for the school Homecoming dance. I was pumped and the school was buzzing about it. The night before the dance we had come from a great church service. They announced the celebration would continue the following night.

I told momma I would pass the dance and go to church. That night it was a football game and I played in the marching band so I had to come. Lang and behold it rained so the band members could go home. I kept hearing about the dance, the music.....the excitement! I wanted to

CHURCH GIRL ON A REGULAR BASIS: Church Girl Goes Takes High School

go. I met up with my bestie Kie and begged momma in front of her friend and daughter. Yes, I was a victim of peer pressure and chose not to fight it off. Momma let me go under the watchful eyes of her friend's daughter, Court, a senior I call my sissy. My mother and brother left me. I stood out in the rain, like a nut, and waited for the game and crowing to end.

I walked in the mud to the gym with my sissy and her friend and cousin. It was cold and wet- which is not a good combination. It was nothing like I imagined. Some people sat in the bleachers, and just watched. My sissy sat down and waited on her other friend. I danced awkwardly! I had to remind myself, I was saved and was constantly watched. I saw girls AND boys twerk.

Boys stood around to watch a big girl jump in a split and twerk. I did clean line dances with a teacher and when music came on that I did not know, I did an old school move. I finally sat down after a while, and that's it! I don't belong HERE! I didn't feel right. I made myself feel like this would be the first party without my momma and I would get wild and have FUN! I didn't. Momma called and I was happy to see her. Momma fussed about me changing my mind on the spot and telling her in front of people. I felt stupid and awful. Then and there I realized I'm a fun-loving- church girl- PERIODTTTT!!! And you know what ? I love it.

CHURCH GIRL ON A REGULAR BASIS: Church Girl Goes Takes High School

CHAPTER 6

The COUNTDOWN!!

So only two more days until Christmas break, today and tomorrow! Exams are going on in the 3rd and 4th block, so I'm leaving at 11:25 am. I only have to take the Biology EOC. I'm not just watching the clock; it's now 10:34 am! Have mercy! Pitiful Christmas music fills the air. Oh, how I wish we would have a Christmas party besides quiet music, a small tree, fake stars, and strings hanging from the ceiling, and pie (π) stocking.

I'm meaning literally, the pie that equals 3.14. Making a difference crosses through my mind every day. Like how in the world will Majayla Ann Page make a change in High School. And I never saw the difference, I was making until now! My smile, language, style, heart, and care share a testimony every day, because girls, whether we like it or not, there is ALWAYS

CHURCH GIRL ON A REGULAR BASIS: Church Girl Goes Takes High School

someone watching you. Whether it's the attention we strive for or the attention we want to run away from. I've been blessed to find the reason why. Its because we claim God and though everyone says they know Him and go to Church on Sundays, do they really claim Him?

"One of the Questions of Life," and what's crazy is that people say that, but do stuff totally left field. Hold up, I answered "one of the questions for life", they don't claim nor want Him. Oh, snap! It's 11:00 am!

TWW-EE-NN-TT-YY-FI-VV-EE MOOORREE MINNNNUUTEES! Ok, back to our subject! My momma constantly tells me that at this age kids don't know what they want to be or who they want. I can truly say I used to be in the confused bunch but no more! I know God made me and loves me! I know I'm a child of the Most High King! I know like boys, puppies, kittens, books, romantic comedies, hot chocolate, Chick-fi-la, Zaxby's Crab legs, and Ham! And whatever God has for me is what I want! And girls, and boys that perhaps joined the talk, I can say wholeheartedly, it's the best state of mind to live in! NEW UPDATE: it's 11:20 am! FIIIIVVVEE MOOOOOORRREE MINNNNUTTESS!!

CHURCH GIRL ON A REGULAR BASIS: Church Girl Goes Takes High School

CHAPTER 7

HAPPY NEW YEAR!!!

> Isaiah 43:19 "See, I am doing a new thing! Now it springs up; do you not perceive it? I am making a way in the wilderness and streams in the wasteland."

So for starters, my Christmas break went great! Some of my family Florida and my cousin Arianna, currently 15, and I got some catching up after a year with no contact. We spent our time talking about her future husband from Mindless Behavior member Princeton and their wedding. I laughed so hard just hearing her talk but how she loves messing with my brother, she practically waits all year for this!

We talk about getting flirted with and how there are no boys our age who love God. But I wonder if church-boys feel the same way because the Bible does say: *Whoso* findeth a wife findeth a good *thing*, and obtained favor of the LORD Proverbs 18:22. Which means men look and seek women. And then I remembered Jerimiah 29:11, which says, For I know the thoughts that I think toward you, saith the LORD, thoughts of peace, and not of evil, to give you an expected end. That reminds me of how lucky I am that even if there is no one in sight right now, my someone is looking for me and out of all God's children, He is thinking of me and that makes me special.

CHURCH GIRL ON A REGULAR BASIS: Church Girl Goes Takes High School

CHAPTER 8

Deuteronomy 3:22 "Do not be afraid of them; the LORD your God himself will fight for you."

Coming back to my High School went better in some ways than others. I've noticed that I can walk in the halls without getting crushed and without constantly telling people 'sorry' for bumping into them. I had my dance recital on Wednesday. I was so excited and happy I was going to do what I loved and people were going to see it; however, the devil swarmed behind the scenes.

Some girls changed under the influence of a crowd if I may say! In other words, they showed their true colors; all the smile and laughs faded away. The girls referred to me as my 'friends' and all the unnecessary criticism, they said about me and blamed it on other students, when I knew it was them talking about me. No big deal right?

CHURCH GIRL ON A REGULAR BASIS: Church Girl Goes Takes High School

WRONG! My friends are extremely sensitive and so like me speaking up, I just knew it was going to backfire. One of my friends cursed those mean girls out that talked about me when I had to teach the class, so bad under her breath! So the whole time we came back from the stage to change clothes, some girls pointed fingers and talked about others. Girls can be simply cruel and evil.

It was obvious that most girls only talked about my friend in order to see how far they could talk about her until she flipped. I tried my best to be that good Christian,friend by singing songs and by quoting my pastor by saying: " We are a TEAM and we work TOGETHER! As I suspected, I was the only one on board.

To be honest, if I was growing deeper in god I would have had some words too. But on the bright side people said we did well. I had a great time because I know what God has done for me. I was struggling with my turns but I was a beast on that stage! HE TURNED IT! While on the way out I hugged my friend whispering to the one that was mad all night, " Don't let people ruin your night." That following week, the last days of the class we had to write a reflection, I told my testimony about overcoming drama, and the fast-paced turns. Girls are still talking about what went on behind stage, but they probably never heard the phrase, "let go and let God" nor the song, 'Let it Go' from the movie *Frozen*.

CHURCH GIRL ON A REGULAR BASIS: Church Girl Goes Takes High School

CHAPTER 9

NEW SEMESTER

Psalm 33:4 "For the word of the Lord is right and true; he is faithful in all he does." (NIV)

So now I have Government and Economics, P.E., English, and Concert Band. Mr. Frank teaches Government and Economics, he's an atheist (he does not believe that there is a God). He has a weird 'spaghetti Monster' hanging from the ceiling in the classroom. I only hope I show boldness for God. I didn't intend to wear cross bracelets but it just happened.

And it just so happened that a girl in my class decided to wear a cross on it too. I told momma and she said she guessed we were all trying to make a statement. As I go into his class, he is really not a bad guy. I don't agree with everything he says – especially when it comes to race- but I have come to realize God loves him too, so why shun him from the get-go? I have decided to pray for him and not argue with him about God. I have decided to prove God lives, and the proof lives by the way I live my life. My smile, my attitude, and my kindness. Momma says God doesn't want us to argue about Him, but to show His love. So when those times come, ignore it! I stand firm in the word of God, that's my hiding place!

CHURCH GIRL ON A REGULAR BASIS: Church Girl Goes Takes High School

CHAPTER 10

WACKY ME!

1 John 3:1 "See what great love the Father has lavished on us, that we should be called children of God! And that is what we are! The reason the world does not know us is that it did not know him."

This whole week I've been feeling very regretful! I felt like I let God down. Like when I was writing to Him and a boy stole my pen and wouldn't give it back; I began to write in anger on 'Our time' (me and the Lord). I didn't cuss or anything like that, but it was rude of me to interrupt our moment. OR the time I was in Government and Economics and my partner was driving me crazy!

I tried to have one of the Fruit of the Spirit , which was long suffering , but my top burst! So I did my 'shut down', which is me not saying ANYTHING! And when I say nothing, you know without a doubt , there is something wrong with me. Then in P.E., the girls and I kind of made a pact to jog slow because we couldn't run. By the time I was only yards away from the finish line, I ran full force and beat them all. But I felt bad because it was like I went back on my word. I asked my friend if they made them, and she said no because I ran track before.

It made me feel better but even in track season I was always in front of the very last runner. But momma reminded me sometimes we blow things up that really don't matter. But in all my wackiness God still loves me and has already forgiven me. Even when I talk too much or doubt Him...He loves me. And that's why I love Him.

CHURCH GIRL ON A REGULAR BASIS: Church Girl Goes Takes High School

CHAPTER 11

I Can't Without...HIM (Jesus Christ)

Isaiah 41:10
"Fear not, for I am with you; be not dismayed, for I am your God; I will strengthen you, I will help you, I will uphold you with my righteous right hand."

So much has happened this semester. My great grandmother died the one me and my momma have been helping to take care of- she had Alzheimer's disease-. I don't know how to comfort my mother because she's taking it hard. And everything I say she says, "It's ok for me to cry, I know she's in HEAVEN, but I want her for myself." We started going to grief groups, with other people that are going through the same thing.

Surprisingly, I found that more comforting to me, even when I try to suppress the sadness I feel of her loss, and to my mom- she smiles more in there than when she is around the family. I

CHURCH GIRL ON A REGULAR BASIS: Church Girl Goes Takes High School

don't know if its because they let her cry , or if she finds peace in the group.... On the bright side of my High School life I'm not getting crushed while I walk through the small halls. And I have mastered packing school books- maybe it's because this new semester required no textbooks, and I have both of my core classes in one notebook-! I expect so much from God, like I want almost everything in the world: lights, fame, fortune, peace, love, and understating.

Because I'm in school I feel that it's not possible, my faith constantly gets weary and I doubt myself and God continuously blesses me! I keep forgetting the God I serve! The creator of the universe, the starter and finisher, king of kings, and Lords of Lords and best of all....my DADDY!

He loves me, He has a plan for me and knows when I slip up and knows when I'm ready for all He has for me! Calling ALL my sistas in Christ let's eliminate fear in all we do, and tell doubt no more from this day forth. Now after that,

CHURCH GIRL ON A REGULAR BASIS: Church Girl Goes Takes High School

it's not easy. I have been trying it all week; it takes work, but it IS possible.

CHURCH GIRL ON A REGULAR BASIS: Church Girl Goes Takes High School

CHAPTER 12

The words To Stand Up, Never Came up.....

Exodus 4:10-13—**And** Moses said unto the **Lord**, O my **Lord**, I am **not** eloquent, neither heretofore, nor since thou has spoken unto thy servant: **but** I am slow of speech, **and** of a slow tongue.

Today, in Mr. Frank's class after watching an Inequality video, the discussion went from money and economy, to react in an instant. He spoke about how police men targeted the minority group- in other words, the African Americans- to be arrested, and give tickets to and say it was ridiculous how 'they' act; so good so far right? Not for long!

A redneck behind me began to say that it wasn't wrong and maybe they didn't mean it. His tone was harsh and forceful. I feel the anger behind my head. Mr. Frank began to say no they meant to say what they did. The boy shouts back, "Did you hear the accident of a white police

CHURCH GIRL ON A REGULAR BASIS: Church Girl Goes Takes High School

officer shooting a black male", and he rushed to say although he was unarmed he did rob the store, which meant that he was 'dangerous'. Then Mr. Frank quickly says, with the class, "Am I saying Michael Brown was a saint?" the class answered back (including me), 'no'. He continued, "Was he a bad person," the class all answered, "yes"; He then adds, "He was a terrible person"! "Did he attack the policemen", he continued, we all answered 'yes'.

Mr. Frank kept going, "I don't understand why people are getting why people are getting 'gone oh' about this, I'm just saying they should have said something about it before this...." HOLD UP! I did not catch it until all was said and done! Michael Brown did not attack the police man; who 's to say he was a bad person and when he was shot more than six times to be exact, and his hands were up!

And I,' Ms. Big Mouth' says nothing! This left my day in regret, anger, and fakeness....(I would smile 2 hours , but would be in deep thought the next 2 hours). Momma told me that I should feel bad because it was wrong, but she said I probably went along with it because I was overwhelmed and shocked and it all happened so fast. Then she explained that's how the devil works when he comes in like a flood. She said I could have a second chance.....Tomorrow.

The next day, while in the library to continue working on our project as I watched him walk, I took a deep breath before raising my hand. I slowly raised my head ready for the fight! " Yes Majayla", he said professionally. I spoke," I would like to make a comment on what you said about Michale Brown." He nodded.

With a business and stern look I add, "What you said was incorrect." "Oh, really," he said honestly, "How so?". I spoke again, "He was shot several times, with his hands UP, and he DID NOT attack." He responded, "Well there is no evidence of that!" He then pulled out a chair and sat and then stated, "Wilson (the police officer) was stupid for what he did. He put himself in that situation, I feel sentimental 'bout it too. I've checked the report, they spent 6 months on the case, but just like the cases in Birmingham, they had some reasons- "I interrupted, " what was those reasons?" He answered, "Did you read the article, referring to all the cases of the people who got arrested, which were all black!" I responded, "No, I did not."

He then said, "Well, read it and it shows the evidence and why they saw them as suspects." I said, "Well, I looked at NBC News and it said that." "Well, there are shades of gray," he responded. I finished the conversation, with "Well, I was very offended." "Oh", he said, "I'm sorry, but you understand what I'm saying?"

I reply with, "yeah, thank you. I see what you're saying "Truly, I see his side, and MINE, but overall, I'm glad God gave me the chance to stand up and speak what was right because I ended up with an understanding and was able to get a point across.

CHURCH GIRL ON A REGULAR BASIS: Church Girl Goes Takes High School

CHAPTER 13

"Thy way, O God, is in the sanctuary: who is as great a God as our God?"
Psalm 77:13, KJV

Lately, I've been having some good days in school, God is truly a blessing. I now like Mr. Frank's class. I noticed this is a class where I can talk and not get in trouble. I also noticed the way society says we're supposed to live. I must do a budget project and with this we see how hospitals make money and how health care works and how student loans and college costs.

It's a lot I'm thinking we should ALL be broke!! It's really eye opening because I get to go out to eat and sometimes get a good home cooked meal and still have lights, go to the doctor for check ups, shop , and have a roof over my head. I am soooo blessed. WE are soooo blessed. God loves us so much that HE not only just lets us get by in life but continues to bless us through our life, when we feel like times are hard, God sweeps us off the dump pile, cleans us up and puts us on top!

What a Great God!

CHURCH GIRL ON A REGULAR BASIS: Church Girl Goes Takes High School

CHAPTER 14

"**Be anxious for nothing**, but in everything by prayer and supplication, with thanksgiving, let your requests be made known to God." Philippians 4:6

So I have been stressing most of February (it's now March!). I have been praying and fasting and put that on "repeat". I want to audition for a role that is not in this state and to me it's pretty HUGE. I claimed to put it in God's hands; I took some time to not eat at lunch and I chose to go to the library instead. But the truth was...I put it all in my hands.

I searched how to submit my own audition papers, I did my own searching for headshots at school and begged others. I went crazy, and then I broke. One day at the mall- of all places- I cried claiming to be nothing, God overlooking me, and being worthless, and asking what was wrong with me.

CHURCH GIRL ON A REGULAR BASIS: Church Girl Goes Takes High School

No matter how many times I received lectures from my mom, and yet still I felt hopeless. As I went to school the following week I fell into depression. It got so bad my grandmother took me aside to give me scriptures to go and study Jeremiah 29:11, "For I know the thoughts that I think toward you, thought of peace and not evil, to give you an expected end."

Doubt was still there... Then in Bible Study, the topic was doubt and how to overcome it. I learned that doubt was fear and to the state of being uncertain. And I asked Ms. MC (a teacher at the school that represents the Lord) for help. She said, "Fear is false, and to kill it, you will have to use truth, which is the Word of God." How crazy am I; God showed me His love over and over to me for the past few weeks and still is!

He gave me teachers, and leaders to come and help ME see the love that He has for me -Beautiful, unconditional love. I finally gave it over to Him and said if He doesn't do it, I know that He can, and I will choose to still believe. Ever since I did that, I got a headshot (by my librarian), and finished my resume (edited by my mom), and it was placed in an envelope and was professionally labeled by my dad, (after begging took place). Happy to say, my information was shipped off. The hardest thing was to let go, and the best thing was giving it to Him.

He is my daddy and my savior; He is the one that loves me even when I doubt and turn away from Him! Surrendering was the best part because I'm finally happy and relieved of the burden I choose to bear alone. It's amazing that my hair is still brown because, after all that stress, my hair should be white!

One week later*

I did not get the callback but that won't stop me from believing…This 'NO' will lead me to my mind-blowing 'YES'.

CHURCH GIRL ON A REGULAR BASIS: Church Girl Goes Takes High School

CHAPTER 15

"...**Though he slay me**, yet will I trust in him: but I will maintain mine own ways before him." **Job 13:15 KJV**

I got the flu and missed school for a week and although there was no time limit to go to bed, it wasn't fun! I missed church and seeing healthy people. Yeah, I kind of got my momma and daddy sink; they weren't too happy either. So the week before spring break I had to catch up with a week's worth of school work. God made a way for me to be on top of things by that Wednesday.

Well, some stuff happened this week. My budget project won Tuesday was due Wednesday and I had a track meet on Tuesday. God made a way for me to wrap up my project the night after the track meet. It looked good and I felt good about it. My board was yellow so while presenting, I wore shades as a way of saying "My future's so bright, you'll have to wear shades!" God gave me

CHURCH GIRL ON A REGULAR BASIS: Church Girl Goes Takes High School

'dat. Everyone loved it- I thought- I got an 81 on the project. I was angry because I did it and not my mother, nor father. I was creative and I was energetic; what's wrong with that!

Later on the same day, my friends who were 16 and 17, Lizzy and Brandon, who really don't get along, were talking in the library. We saw a girl with a provocative dress on, and they both agreed that she was blessed up top...a little too blessed.....more than usual. Which, this really shouldn't matter, but somehow the discussion of judgment came to me!

Suddenly Lizzy pointed at me and said, "do I see a nibble". I was like ' are you really kidding me'; I wanted to scream. First of all, we're in front of my other friend, who happens to be a guy. I felt my face getting red; I was so embarrassed. I can honestly see that Jesus helped me during that.

I replied in shockers, and said, "oh my gosh Lizzy, why would you- Don't look at me!" I wrapped my rain jacket over me in a playful manner. Brandon said nothing, until my playful reply and chuckled. He was gentlemen the whole time. As someone calls for me, I get up and walk away from the table; Brandon follows behind.

We later had our regular laugh-out-loud conversations, which left me on a good upbeat note. As I think back on it, that was an attack from the enemy. Lizzy wouldn't do anything like that to me. And most of the feuds between Lizzy and Brandon almost ended my friendship with Lizzy, I recognize it's an attack too. I will still be her friend, and I will choose to cherish both Lizzy and Brandon.

I say all this to say don't let the devil's attack get in the way of what you KNOW is true. This goes with friendships, God's love, goals, or whatever is hindering you. Recognize the devil, and fight with praise. That night I went to church and shouted for my release, and that's why I can tell my story and know God's got a way that's mighty sweet. Shout for your release and tell your testimony. You never know, it might help somebody find their breakthrough.

CHURCH GIRL ON A REGULAR BASIS: Church Girl Goes Takes High School

CHAPTER 16

"Bless the LORD, O my soul. O LORD my God, thou art very great; thou art clothed with honour and majesty."Psalm 104:1, KJV

This week Good has shown Himself mighty and strong – as always-! It starts off like this: Sunday I was stressed out of my mind! I was unsure of how things would work out with Track and Drum Major practice, being on the same day. The next day, to my surprise, track practice was canceled due to the weather, so I was able to go to Drum Major practice and it went well.

However, even with this miracle, I worried about the home track meet, scheduled for the following day and Drum major practice would be on the same day AGAIN! However, God did it AGAIN, and the track meet was canceled; therefore I was able to go to practice. I really wanted to go to the drum major practice because

CHURCH GIRL ON A REGULAR BASIS: Church Girl Goes Takes High School

the director was planning to teach conducting skills for the marching show and not the basics. The next day, I auditioned for the position; I think I did well. While waiting for my name to be called, I sat quietly and ate chips rapidly. A candidate said, "I like how you're just sitting there like, 'I got this'." A minute went by and they decided to continue, "And I like how you're eating chips. I haven't eaten since Monday!" Another candidate said, "Why? Because you're nervous?" They nodded.

I was the first one to go- probably because I was the youngest-. You talk'n nervous, Lord I was terrified! " You got this!" the current drum major shouts out to me. You see, my brother was the drum major the year before him, and almost everyone assumed that I had received help from my brother.

Well, they didn't know that this whole week he was traveling from Orangeburg to Alabama to Detroit and then back to Orangeburg. So when we talked, the topic was mostly about his well being.

CHURCH GIRL ON A REGULAR BASIS: Church Girl Goes Takes High School

So all my moves were given to me by no other than Jesus Christ!

Afterward, I met my mommy to tell her how it went and I was later dropped off at track practice. We finished at 4:30 pm, so I only had 30 minutes of practice-so no complaints here-. Momma was supposed to make errands out of town; so we went to Belk and shopped and I ate 3 cookies from American Fun Cookies, and then we ate fried chicken, fries, and a salad.

****

I was struggling with a specific song in the band; there's a high note that I can't get no matter how many times I practice. Every time the band played that song, I noticed someone always tilted their head to hear me mess up. I told my momma, and she told me to trick my mind to think that those people were listening to see if I would get it this time; in fact, she said that I would get it the next time. She said to anoint my lips with oil and practice! Proud to say . I actually

CHURCH GIRL ON A REGULAR BASIS: Church Girl Goes Takes High School

hit the high note three times, and that includes a time by myself, with the band, and then with only trumpets! Ain't my God good?! Moreover, the track game and practice was canceled again today, so BONUS!

Now with all these miracles, of course, the devil showed up. When I saw my friend, he was mad and sad; he would tell me what was wrong either. I worried about him and didn't like his silence. After trying to talk, singing songs, fussing, I finally began to pray. I noticed after the prayer he opened up and came to himself. He finally told me what was up- he got mad at ignorant people- and then he smiled at me, I guess he finally let it go.

I told you my 'miracle-filled-week' because I want you to know that God can do it for you- only you know what 'it' is. Yes these issues may be small to somewhat maybe big for me may be small for you, or it can be the other way around- but hey, it's High School! That doesn't matter; I dare you to trust Him (Jesus Christ)! Gosh, I even dare myself! Let's experience those little daily blessings that turn into big miracles. Let's bask in unconditional love, that a heavenly daddy (God) has on reserve for his royal children!

I didn't make drum major but the only boy that audition did. And you know what.......I was happy for him.

■ ▪ ■

CHAPTER 17

Finally, the month of May has come! This is when almost everyone counts down the days that lead to summer! But even with this excitement and relief, a bump always forms on my side of the track. Last month my friend Lizzy completely cut the rope (our friendship). She stopped our regular smiles, jokes, laughs, and greetings altogether. Later I learned this was because I spent a lot of time with my other friend brandon.

I didn't like the way things went down between us. I tried to bring us back together on my own , but that didn't work out. I took it all to God, I couldn't show my friendly love to Lizzy and Brandon , one disliked the other. The next thing I knew, Lizzy wanted me to call her. We talked and it felt refreshing. The following day I found myself sitting among both of them. God repaired my broken chain of friendship....so I thought.

CHURCH GIRL ON A REGULAR BASIS: Church Girl Goes Takes High School

****

Brandon made it on the Marching Band, which means that we will be spending more time together. These past weeks ,I noticed Brandon drifted off to a new crew and soon after Lizzy gained a new bestie. At first, I felt some type of way, like hello; I thought this was our thing! These feelings came for both Lizzy and Brandon.

I'm finally listening to my momma when she said people grow apart; but never let go of your friendships because you are growing up. It's not like I'm totally being ignored, but it's not the same. I guess that's how Lizzy felt when I was with Brandon. I've decided to give time to my ultimate friend, Jesus Christ.

I guess I got so consumed with people and 'friends', in high school, I looked over another ..and possibly...maybe....probably...Ok , I DID look over giving everything, even friendships to Him (Jesus Christ). So as for me, I will give everything

CHURCH GIRL ON A REGULAR BASIS: Church Girl Goes Takes High School

to Him , because He will NEVER change, and our love and friendship has no time limit!!

CHURCH GIRL ON A REGULAR BASIS: Church Girl Goes Takes High School

CHAPTER 18

This was the last week of school, and it went like this:

Monday was Memorial Day and boy did I have myself a good time! Early that morning my mom and I went to perchance something to place on the lawn for the cookout. Soon as we returned my daddy started to grill. My grandma and grandpa came just in time to eat and to take part in the juicy and tender grilled meat fresh salad, to-die-for chili, maple beans, and Ball Park burgers.

I was pitiful, when I had to return to school! The day I returned was the day I found out that I had to take Mr. Franks exam . I was crushed; I thought I was done with that class. My day was gloomy after that. After school, I had marching band practice –lucky me- which lasted until 5:00pm. And then I had to attend the Athletic Banquet. Yes, I survived yet another year of

CHURCH GIRL ON A REGULAR BASIS: Church Girl Goes Takes High School

TRACK! So after being picked up I came home to get dressed for the event, to receive myself an award. My mom and I went and found track people handing out programs and holding the doors. So I greeted people getting their programs, and walked my mother in the gym. During the awards, there was going to be a long wait for them to finally recognize the track 'girls'.

When they finally got to it, I was left sitting there while everyone on my row got up to receive their participation award. Yes, I got nothing! I felt hurt, disappointed and mad; but worst of all I felt like a failure. Momma made me ask why I didn't receive one; The coach said that I didn't come to regionals. Going home I cried, and I announced I was done with track. She said to not allow people to take me to that 'place'. She said God had it under control.

You will never guess what happened the next day. The Track coach came up to me out of the blue, and presented me an award during P.E. My name was spelled right and everything. He told me to shake his hand and 'do it right'. I had exam week and that Monday, I had to take Mr. Franks and my P.E. exam.

While taking Mr. Frank's exam, I know he is a very particular guy, so for the essay section, I had to do so, what I had to do; I left no information behind and wrote about a two page paper for each essay question. Through Jesus Christ alone, and made a 100 on both of my exams! God is AMAZING! I thank God for everything I have gone through because he's an eternal God, and He has sent me here for such a time as this!

CHAPTER 19

...3 years later...

Upon the cares of life, tedious International Baccalaureate courses and assignments, track, and marching band, I was not able to clear my thoughts as usual. However, I saw God's faithfulness EVERYDAY!

I became the first African-American female Drum Major and the First Robotics Captain of my high school both my junior and senior years. And I ended up traveling abroad to Germany, Austria, Switzerland, Paris and Vaduz! It wasn't easy...I went from friends to associates. Turns out Jordan was only my friend because almost everyone knew me, and he thought our friendship would help him get into the band- and to my surprise it did-.

The other girls that I was calling my friends just completely stopped talking to me altogether.

CHURCH GIRL ON A REGULAR BASIS: Church Girl Goes Takes High School

For the first time, my best friend was God. I was lonely in a crowd of people; and the only person that I knew without a doubt was there for me and not to time my downfall, could not be seen but was very present.......His name was Jesus Christ.

I was bullied in the band; imagine that, the leader of the band was talked about and named the biggest joke but the most respected at the same time! Crazy, but true. God's love is so unbeatable and can override any hurt. It pained me to be as social and active as I was, and feel so alone. If you were to watch me from afar, you would think I had it all together, and the one to take the world by storm.

I would volunteer at the Elementary School summer reading program every summer; goof around with the guys on the track team (we would rap and joke around before and after track meets); go to band competitions and catch wins, manage the girls basketball team; go to school make all A's and minister at Fellowship of Christian Athletes meetings, at singing engagements and with a smile and go home to feel like this……..alone and outcasted.

I soon realized that the isolation season was a test and an attack. God was opening doors of opportunity all around me, and even when I felt alone, God was replacing my focus, and trust in people. This season was designed to make me see Him (Jesus Christ), His everlasting love. In that season, I learned to be grateful.

I learned to not look at people because they will love you today and can hate you tomorrow. But there is no love like God's love. His love will NEVER change; even if I change God won't. I am flawed , and yet he calls me perfect! I am dirty, but by His deed on the cross, and the blood that was shed, I AM CLEAN!!

The bible, in 2 Corinthians 12:9. "But he said to me, 'My grace is sufficient for you, for my power is made perfect in weakness.' Therefore I will boast all the more gladly of my weakness, so

CHURCH GIRL ON A REGULAR BASIS: Church Girl Goes Takes High School

that the power of Christ may rest upon me." The Bible also says in Ephesians 1:4-7, 9 KJV:

> ⁴According as he hath chosen us in him before the foundation of the world, that we should be holy and without blame before him in love:
>
> ⁵Having predestinated us unto the adoption of children by Jesus Christ to himself, according to the good pleasure of his will,
>
> ⁶To the praise of the glory of his grace, wherein he hath made us accepted in the beloved.
>
> ⁷In whom we have redemption through his blood, the forgiveness of sins, according to the riches of his grace;
>
> ⁸Wherein he hath abounded toward us in all wisdom and prudence;
>
> ⁹Having made known unto us the mystery of his will, according to his good pleasure which he hath purposed in himself:

Therefore, we are BELOVED, BLESSED, CHOSEN, FREE, and ADOPTED by a KING that LOVES US!

Yes, I am FLAWED, but I am made PERFECT in Jesus! So we are BEAUTIFULLY-FLAWED!! It was until then that I finally realized, my identity

CHURCH GIRL ON A REGULAR BASIS: Church Girl Goes Takes High School

is not in my works, nor is it found in people...it is found in JESUS CHRIST!********

Today, is the last day I walk through these halls. I'm draped with a green gown and a cap in my hand....Its graduation day!! I walked quickly down the hall to the library; call time for the seniors was 5:00 pm, and the program was supposed to start at 6:00 pm. I walked in at 5:30 pm- I had a makeup appointment at 4 and after the artist left I realized I looked dead. So I decided to redo it myself. I was wearing a black crushed velvet dress, and my hair was straightened.

I walked in the library to see all my classmates all in green robes too. Everyone was smiling, laughing, and talking in various cliques; people were grouped in various corners and at different tables. There were the outcast groups; there was a group with basketball, softball, band, baseball and football, and track team members.

I found myself walking around to them all, to hug and to laugh with everyone. I took pictures

CHURCH GIRL ON A REGULAR BASIS: Church Girl Goes Takes High School

with my twin (my one true friend that has the same birthday as me) and associates. I even took a picture with the librarian, after all it would be my final time there as a student, so why not. After I walked away from her, the principal came in. She was a small peptic woman and seemed to be three feet lower than every student; she shouted in the most country-Latta–way, "Alright guys, the time has come. Line up! Quietly."

We all walked back out to the hallway to get into alphabetical order. To my misery and pleasure, I was beside one of my track teammates. We found ourselves, playing around like kids, and having yet another funny debate about life and what our future would look like after this day, and, of course, he picked on me jokily about my height (the dude was a couple of feet over me). I rolled my eyes as usual to his comments, and so did he; he was more flirtatious than usual. We laughed together, knowing it was our last time to be childish.

CHURCH GIRL ON A REGULAR BASIS: Church Girl Goes Takes High School

When the music started, and the line finally moved, I walked into the gym. A cool breeze brisked across my face. I took a deep breath as I finally reached my assigned seat. As boring speakers and students spoke, I stretched my neck to scan the crowd to find my family. To my surprise, my grandpa was on one side with his sister, my grandma, and my brother on the bottom bleacher. Meanwhile, my mommy, daddy, and uncle were on the opposite side of the gym near the top bleacher. The room was packed! I was so happy that they were there, and I couldn't help but smile.

The ushers then came to our row, and I knew it was time to walk the stage. When I finally walked up the stairs and reached the superintendent of the school, He gave me a firm handshake, in return I gave him an energetic smile. He handed me my diploma and it was cold in my hand. As I walked down the stairs, I raised a peace sign; this sign was an act of victory.

CHURCH GIRL ON A REGULAR BASIS: Church Girl Goes Takes High School

P.S.

Dear High School,

You didn't kill me and my scars will heal. I am stronger than ever. I know who I am, and I want to say....Thank you. I leave you with joy, memories, and with completed lessons. I'm going to college. Because you said I couldn't, and God said I could; I want to confirm with you that I DID.

ABOUT THE AUTHOR

Majayla Page is a native of Marion, South Carolina. Her love for writing began at the age of three-years-old. She is a non-fiction story novelist, and aspires to encourage young readers to see God from their level. She loves reading, writing, praise dancing at church, singing and acting. As a queen with three titles [Miss South Carolina princess (2006), Miss Dillon County (2018), Miss Pre-Alumni Claflin University (2019), she mostly cherishes her job as student Chaplain for the CU Class of '22. She loves sharing God's love and serving others, and plans to do so in another way...with a pen.

Made in the USA
Columbia, SC
24 November 2020